NOISY
Neighbors

DOTT COCKEY

To order additional copies of this book, contact:
Xlibris Corporation
1-888-795-4274
www.Xlibris.com
Orders@Xlibris.com

THIS BOOK IS DEDICATED TO

MADISON NOEL SCHISLER

...WHEN SHE IS READY...SHE WILL FLY...

Living on water front land, on a creek, provides a quiet place free of city noises and a calm, soothing environment in which to live. Walking out on the dock in the morning, one can hear birds chirping and sounds of wildlife. It is quite peaceful with the water rising and lowering as the tide comes in and out. The brackish water provides a habitat to many fish, amphibians and birds.

One morning I was awakened early by screeching and shrill sounds coming from the area of the dock. I walked down to the dock to see what WAS THE NOISE. I had a new neighbor, noisy neighbors, two osprey and they were squawking, probably telling me that they were here now and had taken over the pole for the spring and summer. They were standing on a nest .

Ospreys are really hawks, called fish hawks, with mainly black and white features. Their body is light brown underneath, and white and black above. The wings are outlined in black with white spots on them. Their tails, when opened, are fan shaped. An osprey's head is white and black and the beak is bent for attacking their prey.

When they fly their wing pattern is in the shape of an M and their wings beats loudly.

The osprey is a diurnal bird, birds that are active in the daytime and sleep at night. Its diet consists of mostly fish that it catches from a waterway. However, sometimes they eat rats, rabbits, and amphibians.

Osprey mate for life and tend to reproduce around the age of three to four years, if they can find a site on which to build a nest. When osprey mate they have a 3-5 month period to lay eggs and raise their young. The female usually lays two to four eggs, one egg a day or every three days. The eggs are whitish with splotches of reddish-brown on the shell.

The female nests for about five weeks in order to hatch the eggs. The hatched chicks weigh about two ounces. They take flight at about 8-10 weeks old. They must be careful, of course, of eagles and other birds of prey, such as hawks. Eagles and hawks will fight with the osprey in order to get the food . That can lead to a fatal result for the osprey.

For a period of time the North American population of osprey had declined, during the 1950s through the 1960s, due to toxic insecticides such as DDT. The insecticide weakened the egg shell and sometimes made the eggs infertile. However, DDT became banned and the osprey population rebounded in the 1970s.

Several years ago a friend and I built a frame on which osprey could build a nest. We did that to try to increase the osprey population further and to help maintain the present population. The frame was two by two boards nailed together in a square and we stapled rat wire to the boards. We then mounted it on a tall piling installed for the purpose of providing a nesting site for the osprey.

Two years passed and no osprey. Four more years went by and still no osprey. I was very saddened that no osprey had built a home in my created nest.

But then one morning I awakened to a shrill, screeching sound coming from near the badly worn dock. I went outside and walked down to the dock and there I saw two osprey. They were sitting in the nest squawking and screeching at me. YAY, the osprey were here and had built a nest on my pole frame and had settled in for the spring and summer. But I wasn't sure yet. They might be scared away by humans getting too close to the nest. They are particular about the conditions around their nest and very defensive.

The nest of an osprey was quite a mess. The bottom of the nest that my osprey are on is a broken nest that we had made years ago and it became broken in a storm, fell over, and rammed into the shore line bending the nest in half. We had the broken nest put back down into the water and the osprey built on that broken frame. It is full of sticks, a black vinyl bag, sod and other debris that the osprey could find along the shore to build its nest. Sometimes the osprey build a nest of a buoy, a telephone pole, or some object near a waterway.

At times they coeixsist with other birds making their nest quite busy and noisy.

You can hear the birds loud wing beats as it circles AND CIRCLES over the water looking for fish from as much as 100 feet up. Fish are its main sourcrce of food. When it spots a fish in the water it dives down into the water and picks up a fish with its talons. It has griping pads on its claws to hold the fish securely.

One day there was a blue heron on the far shore side which had caught a fish with its long bill. All at once an osprey dived at the heron and took the fish from the heron. It did a lot a squawking and screeching at the heron, probably to scare it and make it drop the fish.

I observed the osprey frequently to try to learn its habits and to enjoy its presence. One day I realized that the osprey had laid eggs and hatched them into living breathing baby osprey, chicks. I was so delighted.

On one occaison the osprey was on its nest squawking and I heard a sound. When it saw me walking that way it began squealing at the babies in the nest and then the chicks made a deep throated sound back, as if to acknowledge that someone was near them, possible danger.

The chicks were fed by the female osprey. She is also in charge of incubating the eggs, and brooding and feeding the chicks. The male provides the food and may be seen standing on the edge of the nest during feeding time to guard the chicks. The male osprey would catch the food, usually a fish, and bring it back to the nest. The female would then break the food apart and feed it to the chicks. Usually the strong chick was fed first.

After the chicks grow and learn to fly they are able to catch their own food, the osprey think about migrating to the south for the winter, to return again in March or April to start the cycle over again. You see them flying around the sky looking for a good place to build a nest, usually in March.

Watching my osprey for the spring and summer, observing their habits, building their stick pile for a nest, hearing their loud squawking noise when someone or another bird gets close to their nest their, seeing them feed and care for the chicks, and feeding their young has been a rewarding experience. They were surely missed when they migrated for the winter. The noisy neighbors were gone until the following spring.

The End